it's Raining Cats and Dogs

An bsession Book

PAT ROSS

VIKING
STUDIO
BOOKS

Also by Pat Ross

Dedicated to the **D**ogs We Know and Love · · ·

Chester	Scotch	Buffy	Rhody	Shadow
Mr. Winnie	Ralph	Lorna Doone	Amber	Yalta
Dixie	Jolly	Paddle	Monty	
Shadow	Patches	Chan	Clementine	
Mufti Malone	Lily	Mikey	Sanders	
Godiva	Daisy	Caesar	Panda	

and in Memory of the **D**ogs We Have Known and Loved · · ·

Muffin I	Puppy	Fergus	Palo
Muffin II	Muppet	Jocko	Harzitz Doodies
Brindle	Spot	Brie	Stella
Shadow	Sam	Raleigh	

Let sleeping dogs lie—who wants to rouse 'em?

Charles Dickens

Major

Born a dog
Died a gentleman

Epigraph on dog's grave

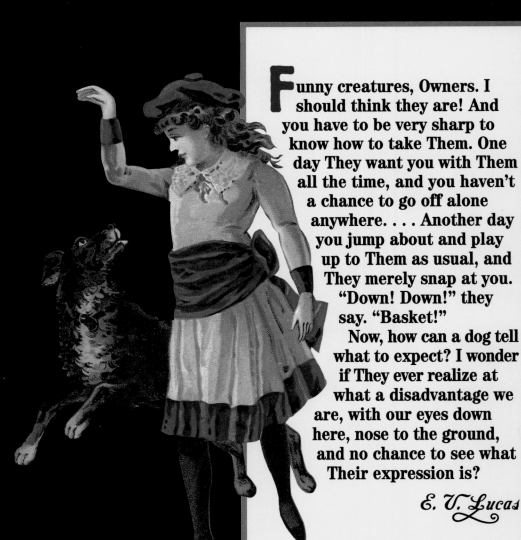

Funny creatures, Owners. I should think they are! And you have to be very sharp to know how to take Them. One day They want you with Them all the time, and you haven't a chance to go off alone anywhere. . . . Another day you jump about and play up to Them as usual, and They merely snap at you. "Down! Down!" they say. "Basket!"

Now, how can a dog tell what to expect? I wonder if They ever realize at what a disadvantage we are, with our eyes down here, nose to the ground, and no chance to see what Their expression is?

E. V. Lucas

The great pleasure of a dog is that you may make a fool of yourself with him and not only will he not scold you, but he will make a fool of himself too.

Samuel Butler

The dog was created specially for children. He is the god of frolic.

Henry Ward Beecher

My little old dog.
A heart-beat at
my feet.

Edith Wharton

Faithfulness and a forgiving spirit are two of the finest qualities in men, and they are the chiefest qualities of dogs.

Your dog is not forever taking offence; he does not know what a slight is; he never believes that you meant to hurt him or could possibly forget him. He licks your hand after you have struck him and shames you if you have struck in anger; he welcomes you home after days or weeks or months of absence; he sympathizes with you when you are sick, and will break his heart for you if you die.

William H. Carruth

A dog's nose is ever cold. *John Clarke*

There is no better companion for a boy than a dog. He stays by you through thick and thin. . . . He will not desert you for the new boy who moves into the house across the street. He will not teach you to be quarrelsome, but he will fight for you to the death.

William H. Carruth

The censure of a dog is something no man can stand.

Christopher Morley

He cannot be a
gentleman which
loveth not a dog.

John Northbrooke

His nose is short and scrubby;
　　His ears hang rather low;
And he always brings the stick back,
　　No matter how far you throw.

He gets spanked rather often
　　For things he shouldn't do,
Like lying-on-beds, and barking,
　　And eating up shoes when they're new.

He always wants to be going
　　Where he isn't supposed to go.
He tracks up the house when it's snowing—
　　Oh, puppy, I love you so!

Marchette Gaylord Chute

Some visitors, you see, dislike dogs; and then one has a perfectly rotten time being kept away altogether or practically confined to basket.

E. V. Lucas

I am the type of dog that should be the only dog in the house, and They ought to know it. If there are dogs that like to share their people's attention with other dogs, let them; but don't ask such nonsense of Aberdeens.

E. V. Lucas

FOR THE SAFETY OF THE PUBLIC.

Every dog is entitled to one bite.

English proverb

Perhaps the final test of anybody's love of dogs is willingness to permit them to make a camping-ground of the bed. There is no other place in the world that suits the dog quite so well.

Henry C. Merwin

We can tell the big things that we so dread, such as Their going abroad, by the luggage. When we see that, we know the game is up. But the smaller excursions They are always making— how can we tell what our fate is to be then? . . . What we don't know is whether we are going too, or not; and it is that terrible insecurity which wears a dog out.

E. V. Lucas

Dog biscuit is
very well
indeed, but should
not be fed oftener
than once a day!

Emily Holt

A lean dog shames its master.

Japanese proverb

One barking dog

The leaner the dog the fatter the flea.

Polish proverb

sets all the street a-barking. *Old saying*

A certain amount of discipline is necessary for a dog. If left to his own devices, he is apt to become some-what dissipated, to spend his evenings out, to scatter among many the affection which should be reserved for a few.

Henry C. Merwin

Perhaps the happiest household to which I ever had the honor of being admitted was one where it was sometimes a little difficult to find a comfortable vacant chair: the dogs always took the arm-chairs.

Henry C. Merwin

Newfoundland dogs are good to save children from drowning, but you must have a pond of water handy and a child, or else there will be no profit in boarding a Newfoundland.

H. W. Shaw

When thieves come, I bark:
when gallants, I am still—
So perform both my master's and mistress's will.

Samuel Taylor Coleridge

The only one unselfish friend that man can have in this selfish world, the one that never deserts him, the one that never proves ungrateful or treacherous, is his dog.

George Graham Vest

The dog will have his day.

William Shakespeare

The cat will meow and

As to sagacity, I should say that his judgement respecting the warmest place and the softest cushion in the room is infallible, his punctuality at meal times is admirable, and his pertinacity in jumping on people's shoulders till they give him some of the best of what is going, indicates great firmness.

Thomas Huxley

The Cat. He walked by himself, and all places were alike to him.

Rudyard Kipling

O cat of churlish kind,
   The fiend was in thy mind
When thou my bird untwined!

John Skelton

More nervous than a long-tailed cat in a room full of rocking chairs.

Old saying

The demeanor of London cats at four a.m. is one of assured freedom . . . in the silver grey of a London dawn they are no longer domestic pets, they are gentlemen at large.

The Spectator

By night all cats are grey. *Cervantes*

A little drowsing cat is an image of perfect beatitude.

Jules Husson Champfleury

Our old cat has kittens three
  And what do you think their names shall be?
Pepperpot, Sootikins, Scratch-Away-There.
Was there ever a kitten with these to compare?
And we call their old mother—
  Now what do you think?—
Tabitha Long-Claws Tiddley-Wink!

Tom Hood

Cats hide their claws.

Thomas Fuller

Cats, like men, are flatterers.

Walter Savage Landor

It's very nice to think of how
  In every country lives a Cow
To furnish milk with all her might
For kitten's comfort and delight.

Oliver Herford

When the tea is brought at five o'clock,
	And all the neat curtains are drawn with care,
The little black cat with bright green eyes
Is suddenly purring there.

Harold Monro

I like the simple dignity
    That hedges round the cat;
You never see her showing off,
    She lets the dog do that.

Talk not to me about your dog,
    It is but idle chat;
Give me that calm philosopher
    Of hearth and home, the cat.

Ruth Kimball Gardiner

A kitten is in the animal world what a rosebud is in a garden.

Robert Southey

I am the cat of cats. I am.
   The everlasting cat!
Cunning, and old, and sleek as jam,
   The everlasting last.

William Brighty Rands

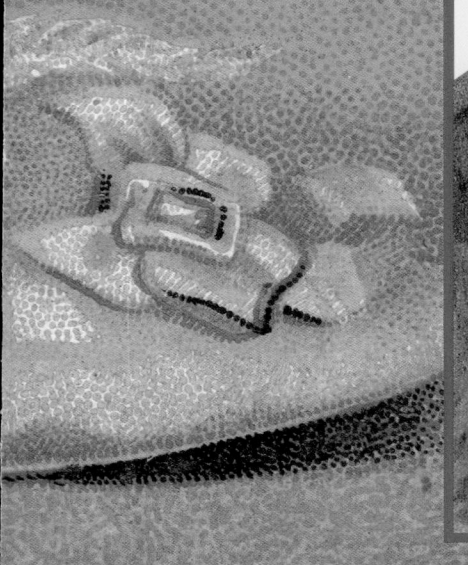

The cat is a dilettante in fur.

Théophile Gautier

The Cat in gloves
catches no Mice.

Benjamin Franklin

When people think that Kittens play,
It's really quite the other way;
For when they chase the Ball or Bobbin,
They learn to catch a mouse or Robin.

Oliver Herford

When the cat's gone
the mice grow saucy.

Thomas Fuller

A good cat deserves a good rat.

Anonymous

What fun to be a cat!

Christopher Morley

If animals could speak, the dog would be a blunt, blundering, outspoken, honest fellow; but the cat would have the rare grace of never saying a word too much.

Philip Gilbert Hamerton

She is dressed in a tortoise-shell suit, and I know that you will delight in her.

William Cowper

y friend Leisa's a cat person. I'm a dog person. For years, we've carried on an affable rivalry over who's better—cats or dogs. Yet I *know* Leisa is crazy about dogs—especially about my dog, Chester. He buries his head in Leisa's tote bag whenever she visits, and digs for treats he's sure she's brought just for him. His favorite toy of the ages—a rag pull resembling a miniature mop that is perpetually wet and slimy and smelling of dog breath—was a gift from Leisa.

And I'm crazier than I will admit to Leisa about cats, especially about her regal yet huggable Maine coon cats, Amos and Eroica. I was once a cat person—owner of the amazing Horrible Hepzibah and the adorable Beautiful Vanilla. Then my new baby broke out with a skin allergy resembling scarlet head-to-toe diaper rash, so our family converted to hypoallergenic terriers. But I still remember how cats must be won over, so I've started growing catnip in my garden. Not to be outdone in the gifts department, I tuck it in my pockets when I visit Amos and Eroica.

Another passion that Leisa and I share is ephemera shows—extravaganzas that sell every kind of antique paper from baseball cards to old picture postcards, plus lots of paper collectibles like early advertising cards, Victorian Valentines, calling cards, and shiny stickers showing cats and dogs doing all the cute and playful things that cats and dogs are famous for. At the close of every show, Leisa emerges with a stack of irresistible pet pictures, and so do I. Then we trade, the way boys do with baseball cards. And I end up with most of the dogs, and she ends up with most of the cats. This book contains our favorites.

Some people say that you're either a cat person or a dog person, but Leisa and I have now settled our small competition by admitting that most of us are *pet* people, who just happen to put dogs first, if you're like me . . . or cats first, if you're like Leisa. So read the dog side first. (No, says Leisa, read the *cat* side first!) Well, you decide.

...How it all began

 **D**edicated to the **C**ats We Know and Love ···

Amos	Murphy	Banana	Shelby	Sadie
Eroica	Pickles	Elvis	Butkus	Popcorn
Molly	Vanya	Ollie	Sinbad	Marshmallow
Tigger	Gustav	Dinky-Do	Smudge	Grover
Mushroom	Fortuna	Maurice	Jade	Bingo
Itsu Bitsu	Joshua	Booboo	Veronica	

and in Memory of the **C**ats We Have Known and Loved ···

Horrible Hepzibah	Scobie	Cleo	Buster
Beautiful Vanilla	Puddin'	Diesel	Tina
Blackie	Missy	Callard	Mercedes
Cuddles	Charlie Brown	Norman	Figaro
Frances	Marc	Cheever	Percy

VIKING STUDIO BOOKS
Published by the Penguin Group
Penguin Books USA Inc., 375 Hudson Street,
New York, New York 10014, U.S.A.
Penguin Books Ltd, 27 Wrights Lane,
London W8 5TZ, England
Penguin Books Australia Ltd, Ringwood,
Victoria, Australia
Penguin Books Canada Ltd, 10 Alcorn Avenue,
Toronto, Ontario, Canada M4V 3B2
Penguin Books (N.Z.) Ltd, 182–190 Wairau Road,
Auckland 10, New Zealand

Penguin Books Ltd, Registered Offices:
Harmondsworth, Middlesex, England

First published in 1994 by Viking Penguin,
a division of Penguin Books USA Inc.

10 9 8 7 6 5 4 3 2 1

Designed by Amy Hill

Grateful acknowledgment is made for permission
to reprint "My Dog" from *Around and About* by
Marchette Chute. Copyright 1957 by E. P. Dutton.
Copyright renewed 1984 by Marchette Chute.
Reprinted by permission of Elizabeth Roach.

ISBN 0-670-85218-X
CIP data available

Printed in Japan
Set in ITC Century Condensed

VIKING STUDIO BOOKS

PAT ROSS

An Obsession Book

It's Raining Cats and Dogs

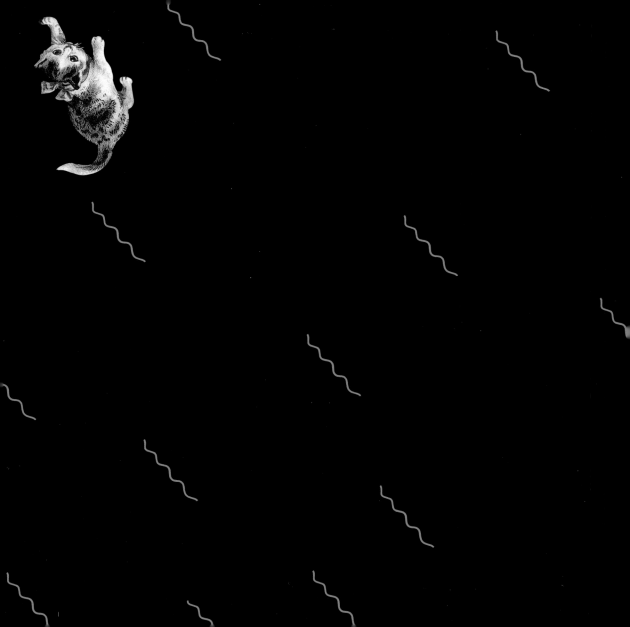